"The way Chandran presents how to become a better leader—not by practicing or doing but by applying and living the three principles—is so true and sets this book apart from others. The concept of saying "this is not your homework" is liberating for the reader. I can look back and see my own personal journey in applying these principles, making mistakes and trying again. Surrendering to just the awareness of the principles is a crucial point to get across."

—Julia Carlson
Founder and CEO, Financial Freedom Wealth
Management Group

"Chandran's wisdom and experience come to light with the generous use of anecdotes, which exactly highlight the nature of the challenges that we face, and help to bring the solutions and their application much closer to home. It gives the reader the sense of being able to address even his or her most intractable issues. A real confidence builder."

—Dominick Garton
President & CEO, Clyde Bergemann Inc.

# Catch

## the

# Arrows

## Simple Steps to Inspire Leadership at Every Level

### Chandran Rajaratnam

**Catch the Arrows: Simple Steps to Inspire Leadership at Every Level**

Published by Leadership Workshops
Copyright © 2019 by Chandran Rajaratnam
All rights reserved.

Leadership Workshops
2288 Liberty St NE
Salem, OR 97301
Email: cr@catchthearrows.com

**Limit of Liability/Disclaimer of Warranty:**

Publishing and editorial team:
Author Bridge Media, www.AuthorBridgeMedia.com
Project Manager and Editorial Director: Helen Chang
Publishing Manager: Laurie Aranda
Cover Design: Funk/Levis & Associates

Library of Congress Control Number: 2019908122

ISBN: 978-1-7331846-0-1 – paperback
978-1-7331846-1-8 – ebook

**Ordering Information:**

Quantity sales. Special discounts are available on quantity purchases by corporations, associations, and others. For details, contact the publisher at the address above.

Printed in the United States of America.

This book is dedicated to the thousands of people who have attended my seminars over the past thirty-three years, many of whom have asked for the content in book form, and to the attendees who have told me that their lives and careers have been enhanced by embracing these principles.

# CONTENTS

# ACKNOWLEDGMENTS

This book would not have been published if it weren't for the support and encouragement of my loving wife, Holli, and my amazing sister-in-law, Julia. Holli spent countless hours transcribing and editing the manuscript as well as reading it out loud to simulate an audiobook to see if it would work in that format. Julia paved the way to connect with a publisher and helped keep the whole process moving. Kudos also to Dawn, my executive assistant from many years past, who first transcribed my seminar speech on these principles. And finally, many thanks to my dear friend Liz who converted my spoken words to written ones while keeping it sounding like me.

# INTRODUCTION

"Leadership and learning are indispensable to each other."

—John F. Kennedy

## When Is It Your Turn?

Leadership can be hard to define, but we know it when we see it. A leader is that person at work who always gets things done, whom people turn to for help, and who seems like a natural choice for promotion.

You may see others in leadership roles and wonder, *How did they get there?* You think you could be a good leader if only someone would give you the opportunity.

You work hard and try your best, but you're not getting ahead as quickly as you'd like. You show up on time and keep your commitments, yet you don't feel like a leader in your organization. As new bosses come and go, you ask yourself, *Will it ever be* my *turn?*

As someone who has hired hundreds of managers, directors, and vice presidents over the years—and I have risen through the ranks myself—I've seen so many people struggle with the same predicament. You think you're doing everything right, but you're not getting the results you want.

What's missing?

Maybe you've just begun your career, and you see people your parents' age working at your same level. You think, *That can't be me thirty years from now!*

Perhaps you're not sure how to realize your potential as a leader in your organization. You tell yourself, *Leaders are just born that way.*

But you may think you weren't born with natural leadership skills, and you've never had the chance to learn them.

## The Secret Sauce

Even if you think you have no leadership skills, your bosses have never seen your potential, and you've tried and failed before, you can still transform yourself into a leader. The change happens when you apply three basic principles to your daily life. I'll teach you those principles throughout the rest of this book.

Practicing the principles revolutionizes the way you approach your job. They work in virtually any setting, from the assembly line to the sales floor to the board room. Putting these principles into action changes the way others see you—and the way you see yourself. You begin to look and feel more like the leaders you have admired in the past.

Best of all, you can start implementing the principles immediately and expect to see results.

My path to discover these key elements of leadership began at my first job as a computer operator and continued until I became senior vice president of sales for Canada's leading retail computer company.

After a meeting with all the store and district managers, two young men came up to ask me how I got where I am. I gave them an answer that was something like, "I've always worked hard and made sure I work on my highest priorities every day. I plan my work and work my plan."

As they walked away, looking pretty unimpressed, it dawned on me. *I didn't really answer their question. They were asking if I had any secrets. They wanted to know*

*the key elements that would separate them from the rest.* I
knew I needed a better answer.

I started to turn the idea around. What type of
person did I want working for me? If I were going to
promote one of them to be a regional manager or vice
president, what qualities would I look for?

I thought long and hard and came up with the three
principles that you will learn in the upcoming pages. I
used these principles as a guide every time I hired someone. I discussed them with my management team, and
I quietly tested my assumptions. In a more official way,
I started to bring these principles to my job in computer
sales and later to two other organizations I led as CEO.

By integrating these principles into the company
culture, I created positive change from top to bottom.
Existing managers took their performance to the next
level. Effective, well-trusted leaders began to emerge
through the ranks.

After teaching these principles for more than thirty
years, I've watched people who never thought of themselves as leaders go on to become frontrunners in their
organizations. I've seen people who thought they would
never get a chance to prove themselves take the initiative and step into leadership roles.

## A Rocky Start

I wasn't granted many advantages in life, but it was my very good fortune to come to North America as a child.

I spent the first nine years of my life in Sri Lanka. When I was two, my mother suffered the unthinkable tragedy of watching her six-year-old daughter die in her arms on the way to the hospital.

A reevaluation of her life's goals inspired my mother to return to university for her master's degree. She then became the first Sri Lankan woman to receive the American Association of University Women Scholarship for a PhD program at the University of Illinois.

I was seven when she came to America to finish her education. We were separated for two long years, and I missed her.

When it was our turn to immigrate, my father and I joyfully reunited with my mom at the Chicago train station on Christmas Eve. She was shocked at the sight of me, not only because I had grown in two years, but also because I was wearing shorts and a light sweater. In Colombo, Sri Lanka, the temperature remains around eighty degrees all year, and I owned only summer clothes. I'll never forget that chilly arrival in the States and the shock of my first winter here.

My parents were educated, but they had to work hard to establish themselves in a new country. Not long after we settled in Canada, my mother developed brain cancer and, over the course of a few years, lost her cognitive abilities. She died when I was fifteen years old.

My father did his best to raise me, but he struggled to keep a job and often tried to make up for lack of money by gambling at the horse races. He died when I was twenty-nine.

Perhaps my tumultuous upbringing led me to be driven and make something of myself. I fully dedicated myself to my career.

I was fortunate that my first full-time job was at IBM in Canada, which gave me good training and opened up career options. First, I worked as a computer operator, which in those days meant sticking pieces of cardstock with punched holes into a computer or labeling reels of memory tape and placing them into storage. After proving myself there, I was promoted to a sales job and eventually into sales management.

After fourteen years, I left IBM to join Computer-Land Canada in the early 1980s. At the time, PCs had just come out on the market, and the only way to buy one was through two competing store chains—ComputerLand and Computer Innovations. When I joined a ComputerLand franchisee, I was the operations and sales vice president, and there were seventeen stores. Over the next two years, I helped grow the company into twenty-seven stores.

I used to think I continued to be promoted because I worked long hours and had drive. Then I discovered these three leadership principles and realized that they had driven my success all along. Through trial and error, I had learned to apply these principles in my jobs. They produced not only excellent results in business but also real personal satisfaction as a leader.

I worked my way up into a leadership role based on what I did, not who I am. For that reason, I am sure anyone else can achieve this same level of success.

## Pay It Forward

Today, I'm the president and a stakeholder at at a fast-growing entrepreneurial company. Before my current position, I was a coach, consultant, and CEO of a few large companies. One thing has remained the same for me in all my professional roles: I truly enjoy helping people, whether it's in their developing careers or in their personal challenges. I slow down and pay

attention to each opportunity to help others; I find that
so rewarding.

I'm not alone in wanting to share what I've learned
about success in business. Many such books cycle
through the retail shelves, and it can be confusing and
overwhelming to know which ones will really help.

Consider this: As a corporate leader and business
coach, I have taught these principles and observed the
results for more than thirty years. I have watched others
listen and question, and then enact and embody these
ideas. People from all walks of life have used the principles in this book to become leaders in their organizations and their lives.

I remain deeply gratified that when people really
embrace these principles, they experience profound
and positive results. After seeing impressive outcomes
from so many of the people I have coached, I offer these
insights with confidence that they will work for you,
too.

## How to Read This Book

Reading this book should not be complicated.

I recommend starting with chapter 1 for grounding
in the elements of leadership and a quick overview of

the three principles. From there, the chapters can be read in any order. The principles are not interdependent and don't need to be implemented in sequence.

I would begin with the principle that you feel will make the biggest difference in your life. After you've got a handle on that one, add the others one by one. Even implementing one or two of the three principles will benefit you professionally and personally.

The more you practice and make these steps part of your regular approach to work, the more you will be seen as a leader by your bosses and coworkers. I think you will find that once you fully embrace these principles, there's no going back. You won't be able to imagine conducting yourself any other way, and you won't want to!

## Prepare to Meet Your Inner Leader

The leadership principles in this book are especially relevant if you are in a sales or customer service job. But even if you don't have a job like that, I have found the principles provide benefits for everyday situations. Parents, team members, volunteers, athletes, families, and community members have all seen positive results in their lives by embracing these ideas.

The principles work whenever there is a task to be done, a goal to accomplish, a promise to keep, an opportunity to be a positive role model, or a chance to build a better relationship.

This isn't going to be complicated, but it also won't be easy. I assure you it's worth the effort.

I have seen the change happen in so many people over the last thirty years. Now, it's your turn to become the leader you aspire to be.

*Chapter 1*

# OVERVIEW

"The pessimist complains about the wind. The optimist expects it to change. The leader adjusts the sails."

—John Maxwell

## The Angry Customer Knows Best

In 1974, I was twenty-six years old and working as an IBM sales rep. We sold typewriters with a feature that stored what was typed on magnetic cards so future changes and edits could be made without retyping the whole document. This made them the hottest thing in word processing technology at the time, if you can imagine.

I had sold five of these machines, and they were

scheduled to be delivered on a Monday. The week before, I confirmed with the customer that they would arrive at her office the coming Monday morning.

On the Thursday before the delivery, we had a snowstorm. It was Canada, after all. On Monday, my customer called me to say the typewriters had not arrived. When I checked into it, I found out that the distribution center had stopped shipments due to the storm. The machines had not even shipped until Monday, so it would be another couple of days before they arrived.

When I called my customer back and told her the news, she was very angry. She had scheduled training for that afternoon, and she now had five people sitting in a classroom with nothing to use.

I explained to her that I couldn't control what our headquarters did, what happened with the weather, or the shipping schedules. She was not satisfied with my explanations.

A couple of weeks later, she called and asked me to lunch. I was relieved. I assumed she was no longer upset, and I thought I could smooth things over by having the company pay for her meal.

I was wrong.

Over lunch, she gave me a stern lecture. She said

that I could not use weather, shipping, or the company as an excuse. I should have checked the day of the snowstorm to make sure the typewriters would be delivered on time. I had promised her they would be there, and they should have been there.

It hit me like a ton of bricks: she was 100 percent right!

I was the one who had said the shipment would be there on Monday, and I'd just assumed everyone else would do their part. I didn't do everything possible to ensure we would deliver the machines on time. I could have double-checked the delivery status and, at minimum, immediately advised her about the delay on Friday morning.

It was so easy to make excuses, but they didn't help the situation. Since then, I have learned that excuses like these *never* work. I also understood that I had broken my promise to the customer. I had said the typewriters would be there on Monday, and that meant I should have done everything I could to make sure they got there on time or at the least informed her with enough warning to reschedule the training she had planned.

Learning from her feedback, I changed how I did things. Although I didn't know it at the time, this is when I actually started applying the three leadership principles to my interactions with customers and others in my life.

## The Best Principles Are Simple but Not Easy

Most important things in life are quite simple. When a group or business is in trouble, people often say, "We have to get back to basics!" I find that less is more, and "more" often makes things difficult to put into practice.

Early in my career at IBM, I read a book called *Executive Qualities* by Joseph Fox. I had the drive and interest in pursuing this track, so the title caught my attention. The book explained twenty-two traits of a successful executive. I read number one. *Yeah, that's me.* And number two—*yep, also me.* Then I got to numbers three and four. *Hmm, those aren't quite me.*

I started to get discouraged. The list of qualities was so long! I figured I had two choices. I could trust this book and give up on becoming an executive, or I could throw away the book and figure things out differently. Perhaps if I had chosen to believe I was missing all the traits I needed to be an executive, I'd still be selling typewriters!

What if I told you, you will lose weight if you follow these fifty-five steps, but you must follow *all* the steps? You intuitively know this won't work because it's too complicated. We know that diet and exercise are the way to lose weight—simple, but not easy.

Let's say you don't like to exercise, but you also don't want to give up your favorite foods. I am like that, too. I love pancakes, bacon, a nice steak, and don't forget about lobster covered with butter. And dessert! Apple crumble with ice cream . . . but I'm getting carried away.

If you want to lose weight and don't want to give up your favorite foods, serve yourself what you like, then draw a line down the middle of the plate and throw half the food away. You will probably lose weight.

It's simple, but is it easy? No way. Throwing away half an apple crumble is painful even to write about. The point is, the best answers are often simple but not easy. They require commitment and determination.

Leaders possess admirable qualities—probably even more than twenty-two of them. Trying to embody all those traits will wear you out. Likewise, comparing yourself with leaders you admire can be discouraging. There's a better way.

My three principles give you a clear, actionable map

from your starting point to leadership. The process is quite simple, but, like all worthy goals, it requires hard work. Let's start by looking at where you're headed.

## What Do Leaders Look Like?

I often ask the people in my workshops to name famous leaders. It's interesting how often the same names come up:

- **Political leaders:** Presidents Obama, Lincoln, Washington, Roosevelt, Trump; Prime Minister Margaret Thatcher; Eleanor Roosevelt

- **Business leaders:** Bill Gates, Lee Iacocca, Warren Buffett, Steve Jobs

- **Spiritual or religious leaders:** Martin Luther King Jr., Mother Teresa, the Dalai Lama, Billy Graham, Gandhi, Jesus

- **Media leaders:** Oprah Winfrey, Terry Gross, Walter Cronkite

What are the attributes that set leaders apart? I'm not saying that every attribute needs to be applied to each individual, but what words come to mind for you? Here are some that have commonly come up during workshops:

- Accomplished
- Influential
- Risk-taking
- Exceptional people skills
- Authoritative
- Critically thinking
- Passionate
- Compassionate
- Change-making
- Can-do
- Confident
- Innovative

Take a look at this list. Are there any other people who also need these attributes to be successful? I think so: anyone who wants to lead. That includes fathers, mothers, coaches, teachers, managers—in other words, all of us!

I want you to look at this list and remember a time when you demonstrated one of these qualities. Now, envision somewhere in your life where you want to show up with new leadership qualities. Perhaps it's a project in your neighborhood, at your sales or customer service job, or on a work team.

What top two qualities speak to you as areas for personal growth? Write these two qualities down.

I'm not asking you to work on these attributes; that would be frustrating. Instead, this is what I suggest: live by the three principles laid out in this book, and you will begin exhibiting these qualities.

When you act on the principles in this book, you'll find that leadership attributes show up anyway.

## Comparisons Defeat Us

While role models can inspire us, it's important to resist making comparisons.

A psychological cop-out happens when we hold ourselves up against a billionaire, a president, Mother Teresa, or any larger-than-life person. When we compare ourselves with others, especially someone "big," we can easily let ourselves off the hook and settle for the status quo. Of course we're not going to match the greatness of a historic figure, but that doesn't mean we should give up on achieving our personal best.

Plus, these kinds of comparisons aren't really fair. Some leaders are born into privilege and precedent. Life would certainly be different for you if, for example, you were part of the Kennedy family. Imagine you were John F. Kennedy, and you decided you wanted to work at a local convenience store. Do you think your dad, Joseph Kennedy, would let you pursue that career path?

Even if you weren't born into privilege, you can still be a leader in your corner of the world. Whether it's in your career or as a parent, Boy Scout Troop leader, or volunteer, you can shine as an exceptional leader in almost any venue.

Heritage or upbringing can give you an advantage in career choices and monetary assets. But it doesn't give you any advantage in leadership. We all have natural-born talents. We all have innate leadership potential. We can all learn principles and behaviors that will make us leaders. I'm asking you to believe in your potential.

## The Three Principles of Leadership

When you commit to these three principles, you will start to behave differently, and then you will just *be* different—a leader. You'll know how to make a bigger impact in your job or wherever you contribute, and you will gain new confidence, skills, and leadership qualities.

## 1. *Catch the Arrows*

When you catch the arrows for your organization, it means you courageously accept responsibility for problems rather than passing the blame to others. This is most relevant to people in customer service, but it applies to anyone who copes with complaints, problems, or miscommunications. If you take responsibility for the issue, rather than point the finger, you empower yourself, protect your organization, and please the customer.

## 2. *Walk the Talk*

No doubt you have heard some version of this principle before, but here's my spin on it. Walking the talk means keeping your promises and leading by example. Often, knowing when you're responsible is just as important as fulfilling your promise. I'll show you how to practice this principle at work and in a way that will get you noticed and valued by your organization.

### 3. *Own the End Result*

Lots of people love to talk about the *process*. This principle forces you to look beyond it. When you focus on the process to the exclusion of the big picture, you paint yourself as a follower, not a leader. Leaders always care about the end result, investing themselves in the final outcome regardless of their control over the variables that go into it. Your CEO is focused primarily on the end result; you'll be more valuable as an employee if you are, too.

These three principles represent a fundamental shift in your mindset that will open up multiple avenues of self-improvement. They are like the elements of good form that give you that champion golf swing. They must be practiced, their nuances understood, before you truly unlock their potential. But once you start to live them, a cascade of positive changes follows.

When you put these concepts into practice, you become the kind of person whom others call a leader. You feel the change in yourself—the pride and confidence that come with knowing you've done your best, and it was good enough. You also feel the change in the way you're perceived in the world. Don't be surprised if you're singled out as a star performer, asked more often for your opinion, or given that sought-after project at work.

I have done it, and I've helped hundreds of others achieve their goal of becoming strong leaders. I can't wait to show you how these principles will revolutionize your world, too.

*Chapter 2*

# CATCH THE ARROWS

"Action springs not from thought, but from a readiness for responsibility."

—G. M. Trevelyan

## The Blame Game

When I was the CEO of a technology company called Softchoice, I lived in Connecticut, but the company was headquartered in Toronto. I commuted to Toronto for a few days every week. At the Toronto office, they wanted to set me up with a private office near the rest of the executives. I said, "No, don't do that. Just put a cubicle in the middle of Inside Sales for me."

You see, I love to hear what's happening with customers. I've always recognized that the happiness of the customer is key to the success of an organization. Inside Sales were the people who took all the orders and answered customer questions.

After a while, these Inside Sales people forgot I was sitting in my cubicle, and I heard everything that went on. As a whole, the customer service provided by our Inside Sales group was top notch. We were growing, and our customers were happy. However, once in a while I heard the reps say things like, "The vendor didn't ship it." "It's stuck at customs." "FedEx missed delivery." "The weather delayed everything."

These customers had ordered a product, and they were calling because they had not received their item as promised.

## Catch the Arrows

As a customer, I'm sure you've had this type of conversation.

Look at these responses. What do you hear? Excuses, passing the blame, even blaming the company. Another classic response from customer service is that there is nothing the rep can do; he or she is powerless to help.

These statements are all true, but they will do nothing to satisfy the customer. They are intended to make sure the customer knows that the sales rep is not the one who caused the problem. These excuses leave customers frustrated or worse.

What should those Inside Sales people have done? They should have "caught the arrows."

You probably get an immediate picture of what it would look like to catch an arrow coming toward you. Let's sharpen that picture. You're out in front of your organization, wearing armor and heavy gloves. The enemy is shooting arrows. You stand there, reaching out to catch each arrow, jumping for them if necessary. No arrow gets by you.

The arrows represent blame, accusations, conflicts, something going wrong, an unhappy customer, or a situation you would rather not face. Catching the arrows means you are solid, strong, and capable. It takes courage to face arrows.

Catching the arrows for your organization also empowers you and serves the customer well. The reverse—transferring the blame—diminishes your power and poorly serves the customer. When you take the hit and cope with the problem, you become a leader. When you catch the arrows discreetly, even secretively, you become a next-level leader.

It may feel unnatural and downright unfair to

accept blame if it's not yours, but it's often the right thing to do.

## We Learn Early to Speak Truth and Blame

Put yourself in the shoes of a sales rep at Softchoice. Imagine you are listening to a customer who is frustrated or even angry. It's not fun to be on the receiving end, right?

When you are the recipient of this anger, conflict, or accusation, it's easy to take it personally and become defensive. It's easy to let that arrow go whizzing right by you into the organization. After all, it's not your fault, and it feels out of your control.

It's human instinct to respond this way.

Let's say as a child you're playing ball with Tommy, and he throws the ball through a neighbor's picture window. The neighbor calls your parents to ask who did it.

You and Tommy were both playing ball; that errant throw could have been yours instead of your friend's. If you take responsibility, your dad will make you give up months, if not years, of allowance to pay for this window. You'll also face painful parental disapproval and anger.

Because, truthfully, you weren't the one to break the window, this is a no-brainer. You say, "It wasn't me; it was Tommy."

Back in my sales rep days, the angrier the customers became, the more personal it felt. I wanted to tell them, "It wasn't me; it was Tommy!"

Taking the hit—claiming the responsibility—is the harder road. But the alternative—letting the arrows go by—will damage your organization.

## A Tale of Two Ticket Agents

Every time you transfer the blame, you are diminished in the eyes of the angry party.

Just as when you were a child, you're only telling the truth to make sure everyone knows you weren't the one who caused the problem. But you're also communicating that you have no power to help. You are useless to the other person.

When I was with ComputerLand, we merged with our competitor and had 102 stores. Some stores were now too close together, and we had to close a number of them. Before making any decisions, I visited every single store, traveling for more than two weeks straight.

It was getting toward the end of my trip, and I was exhausted. My next leg was Moncton, New Brunswick, to Halifax, Nova Scotia. This was back in the days when air travel required paper tickets. Half an hour before departure time, I walked up to the ticket agent at the gate to check in. The agent looked at her computer screen and said, "I don't have you on this flight."

"What do you mean?" I replied. "Here, my ticket even shows 'confirmed' on it."

"Yes, I see you have a valid ticket, but you're not in the computer."

"I don't understand."

"Your travel agent didn't put you in the computer."

"So, what can you do?"

She finally looked up at me and replied, "You have to call your agent."

It was ten o'clock at night, and obviously my travel agent would not be available. The ticket agent said the next flight was overbooked. When I raised my voice in disbelief at this turn of events, she played her blame card.

"Sir, it's not my fault. It was the travel agent's error."

I was incredulous, furious, thinking, *You can't do*

*this to me!* I wanted to talk to her boss and the airline president to give them a piece of my mind. This agent had told the truth, in order to pass the blame, but in doing so she had enraged her customer. She wasn't concerned about the customer's problem. She was happy to have a "good" excuse that showed she wasn't at fault.

If you are on the receiving end of somebody's anger, even if you did not cause the problem, you will lose every time you pass the blame. In the many years I have tested this principle, I have found no exception to this rule. Passing the blame always reduces your power. It lowers you in the eyes of the person you're dealing with.

Unfortunately for me, I had the same predicament on a trip I took several weeks later. But this experience proved the complementary point, that catching the arrows empowers you and pleases the customer.

This time, I walked up to the gate and gave the agent my printed ticket stub, and she typed my information into her computer. She looked puzzled and then called someone. She read my ticket locator code over the phone and said things like, "I don't see it."

*Here we go again*, I thought, already feeling my frustration.

The agent looked at me and said, "Mr. Rajaratnam, I'm terribly sorry. You have a valid ticket, but we don't have you on this flight. We've really made a mistake. I know this is not what you want to hear. You're a great customer of ours. I really apologize, but we're already overbooked on this flight.

"The best I can do is get you on the next available flight first thing in the morning. We'll put you up in a hotel. Again, I know this is not what you want to hear. I truly apologize for this unexpected inconvenience."

This time, I wasn't angry. I didn't feel the urge to call up the airline president. I believed that this agent would help me with anything that she could do. In fact, I was so impressed with the service I received, I tried to hire her!

I knew she wasn't the one who had caused the problem, but she still took ownership of it. She took the arrows for the company, and possibly even our travel agent, and she didn't pass the blame.

Trying to avoid blame by providing the accurate details can feel logical and fair, but it's not the act of a leader. Leaders catch the arrows coming in their direction, whether or not they caused the conflict. This takes courage, but it empowers you and almost always results in a better outcome for your arrow-slinging enemy.

## Catch the Arrows Secretly

An even more challenging way to catch the arrows, one that is absolutely worth the effort, is to catch them in secret.

In this scenario, you act the part of hero, facing down adversity and solving problems without looking for recognition. Make no mistake, heroes inevitably get rewarded, but they don't go looking for the spotlight.

When I worked as president of Gestetner, a company that sells photocopy machines, I used the services of a travel agency that did great work for us. The president of this company knew I enjoyed talking about my three principles, and he invited me to come talk to their agents. I showed up at their office and gave my talk. Right up front, I mentioned how much I loved the customer service they provided. I had selected their agency for all of our employees across the country.

At the end of my talk, I opened things up for discussion. These agents talked about a dramatic example of customer service they were very proud of. They had a customer who had moved to California (the agency was located in Connecticut) who had purchased tickets to go on vacation to the Caribbean.

This was again in the days before e-tickets, when

paper tickets needed to be physically in the hands of the customer for any flight. Because of last-minute changes to these tickets, the agency needed to courier them to California by air. Then, a blizzard hit the Northeast. Boston, Hartford, and all three New York City airports shut down.

The resourceful agents found out that Philadelphia was still open. So an agent with a four-wheel-drive Jeep spent eight hours driving through snow and gridlock to the Philadelphia airport. He got the tickets onto an airplane, and they were delivered to the customer just in time for him to make his flight out of Los Angeles.

"Wow, that was amazing," I said. "Did you tell the customer that story?"

"Oh, we sure did!" the agent replied enthusiastically. "We wanted him to know what good service we provided."

Here's where they made their mistake: they wanted credit for catching the arrow.

Let's think this through. I'm a customer in California, and you just told me what heroic efforts you went through to get me the tickets that I paid for before my flight. I understand it was an ordeal for you, but if I pay a travel agent for tickets, shouldn't I expect to get them?

As the customer, I might think, *They made a point of*

*letting me know how hard this was for them. What if, the next time a blizzard hits, they choose not to perform these heroic efforts? They might give me their normal effort. They could say, "Hey, there was a situation out of our control with the weather." For my next trip, I'd better switch to a local travel agency.*

Imagine the alternative. What if the agents had said nothing? The customer is on his way to the Caribbean when perhaps he sees the *New York Times*. He reads that all the airports near the agency have been closed for three days. Now he's curious. He wonders, *They got me my tickets on time. How could they have done that?*

Out of curiosity, he calls and asks how you managed to get him his tickets with all the airports closed. Now, the answer becomes, "Sir, getting tickets to customers is normal operating procedure. Weather doesn't stop us; airport closures don't stop us. We are your travel agency, and we make sure you get your tickets."

Now, you've got him for life. He's telling everybody, "No matter where you are in the world, deal with this travel agency! The impossible is just standard practice for them."

See the power of catching arrows in secret?

The employees at this travel agency caught the arrow of adversity—a blizzard—and did everything in their power. They could have blamed the weather, but they didn't. They figured out what they could still do, and they did it.

But—and this is the disappointing part of the story—they let the customer see into the internal workings of the company, undermining their exceptional actions. If they had caught the arrows in secret, they might have cemented that client's loyalty rather than planting seeds of doubt.

## Start Your Arrow Collection

Practice catching the arrows by accepting blame, even when it's not your fault. Be willing to take the hit and do everything you can to make it right. Avoid excuses and blaming others or circumstances.

Please work hard not to take criticism personally. Just be there for the other person. You'll notice a shift in tone and attitude when you get rid of the finger pointing and try to help.

Remember that we have all been conditioned, by our parents or through society, to speak the truth and not take the blame for someone else's errors. Of course, we should always tell the truth, but providing details intended to show that you weren't to blame will always make you smaller.

It's difficult to unlearn this practice. It helps to be curious and constructive about the person's problem rather than dwelling on who's at fault.

When I was faced with an angry customer, I learned to defuse the anger before discussing the issue. First, empathize with the customer and the cause of his anger. Then, ask open-ended questions to find out what should have happened, what did happen, and what would solve the problem going forward.

There doesn't need to be any conversation about who made the mistake or what circumstance caused the service failure. When a customer asked me what went wrong or who made the mistake, my reply was, "Let's solve the problem first. We will investigate internally to prevent these issues from recurring."

The customer's priority is to have the problem solved, not to have blame assigned.

Catching the arrows takes courage; doing it secretly takes restraint and maturity. These may feel in the moment like thankless tasks, but I assure you that they pay dividends over and over in your career. Owning a problem and setting it right makes you a leader in your organization.

If you stop reading here and just practice this one principle, you'll find it changes your life. I consider this the most powerful of the three principles.

Catching arrows is about using the right words when you're under attack. In the next chapter, I talk about the power of your actions. When you align your actions with your words, you change how people perceive you.

*Chapter 3*

# WALK THE TALK

"Well done is better than well said."

—Benjamin Franklin

## Why You Fire Your Best Guy

When I first became the president and CEO of Gestetner, the photocopier company, I introduced some values I thought were important:

- Delight the customer

- Treat all people with respect

- Never compromise our integrity

I believe in this level of customer excellence because I have learned that it causes a ripple of positive effects.

I wanted our customers to experience being not just satisfied but delighted with our service.

We created a training program to get all new hires up to speed on our values and practices, and we taught them how to truly delight the customer. We were committed to helping everyone succeed as employees in the company.

However, there were two things that we would not teach: integrity and respect. I had zero tolerance for lying, cheating, and stealing. I insisted that everyone be given respect, whether it was the janitor, the FedEx deliveryman, your coworker, or your boss.

One day in a management meeting, a VP told me about an integrity issue. A sales rep, who was struggling at only 50 percent of his quota, had forged a customer's signature on an order. One of his customers had said he would ask his board to approve an order the following week. Because the rep had not reached his quota, he thought he'd record the order and hope that the customer's board approved it. Well, it didn't get approved, and the order was canceled.

All the managers discussed it, agreeing that this fellow might be in the wrong line of work. He had always been a low performer, and now he'd violated the company's commitment to integrity. They recommended we fire him, and I approved.

Four months later, this same team told me about another integrity issue: they had caught a sales rep forging a customer's initials on a delivery slip.

The sales department was holding a national installation contest. A lot of orders had been placed, but people kept delaying their installation (and we didn't get paid until the machines were installed).

On the last day of the contest, this rep needed one more installation to win. But his customer didn't want the copier installed until the following week. Our rep took a copier and put it in the back of his station wagon, pretending that the customer had taken it. Then he logged it as an installation for the contest. The following week, when he tried to install it, the customer canceled, and the rep had to bring the machine back.

When I asked the VP what he wanted to do, there was a visible struggle on his face. "This is tough," he said. "He's our top sales rep of the year. He performs equal to or better than half of the Philadelphia sales reps combined. He's at 150 percent of quota and a really good guy."

The VP recommended that I give him a stern warning that would go in his file.

I understood where my VP was coming from. But I asked him to look at how that decision would play across the company. We'd be telling our employees that if you're at 50 percent of quota and you cheat, you will be fired. If you're at 150 percent of quota and you cheat, you'll get a warning.

That's not walking the talk; that's changing the walk for each case and not being consistent as a leader. I looked around the room, and I could see the realization hit them.

We fired him, and it hurt. The VP of sales just about had a heart attack. But it's the best intervention I ever made. We did not have another problem like that. If the company would fire the sales rep of the year for something that did not cost the company any money, everyone knew we were serious about integrity.

## Walk the Talk

You've probably heard some version of this principle before. Back in 1963, football great Vince Lombardi said, "Some talk the talk, but few walk the walk." It is wisdom that's been phrased many different ways:

- Say what you mean, mean what you say.

- Practice what you preach.

- Put your money where your mouth is.

Back in 1985, when I started to use "walk the talk" as one of my principles, I had never heard anyone else use this phrase. The principle came to me with full clarity when I thought about the example that leaders set for others. I saw that leaders must walk the talk. Our speech and actions must match.

Walking the talk is the easiest of the three principles to understand, but it is perhaps the hardest to do consistently. It best exemplifies strong leadership. There's nothing that inspires respect like seeing someone act according to his or her principles. And nothing erodes respect like seeing someone talk one way and act another.

I like to think of walking the talk as keeping promises and assuming responsibility. We'll look at what constitutes a promise and how to know when you're responsible. But first, why is your walk so important?

## People Notice Only the Walk

People know who you are by your actions. It doesn't really matter what you say; it's all about what you do.

Have you ever been in a group conversation when someone says, "You know, I'm always like 'this' when 'this' happens"? Then after the person leaves, someone in the group asks, "Who is he kidding?"

If somebody's walk is different from the talk, what do you believe? Only the walk, right?

Let's say a manager declares to her team that a particular issue is critically important. You are a new employee and think, *Okay, it's important. We've got to get on it.*

But a long-term employee corrects you. "For now, it's a waste of time to do anything. If her boss writes to her and then she copies us on the email, *then* we know it's important and should start working on it."

Imagine the reverse. Your manager says to the team, "This is really important, so we need to get this done." Your team member looks at you, the new employee, and says, "She never says it's important unless it's very important. We'd better do this tonight."

As a leader, wouldn't it be wonderful to have that type of impact? When you want to get something done, all you have to do is say the word, and it gets done, because everyone knows you mean it. Imagine the productivity you inspire when you say what you mean and mean what you say. It has a powerful effect!

Perhaps you had a mom who said, "Just wait until your dad gets home. You'll be in big trouble!"

But you learned that when Dad gets home, if you sit on his lap and kiss him, he just melts. You know to ignore your mom's warning.

I had the blessing of raising six girls. My next book will be *Six Ways* Not *to Raise Children*.

I'm kidding. I'm blessed to have daughters and stepdaughters who are kind and caring and making their way successfully through life. However, it's true that my most challenging opportunities to walk the talk were experienced as a parent. If you say that you're going to follow up on bad behavior and then nothing happens, kids catch on very quickly.

The walk is all the child remembers, so it's all that counts. Children naturally push boundaries to learn what's real and what's not. We're not much different as adults. We test and watch to understand who people really are.

It's easy to notice this hypocrisy in other people, especially your parents! It's tougher to take a clear-eyed look at ourselves and see our own contradictions. If you make a full commitment to walking your talk—where your actions and words are consistent—you will feel the difference.

One of the easiest ways to start down this path is to stop making statements about what you are going to do. When you make threats about future discipline for children or statements about what projects you are going to accomplish at work, you risk not doing what you said. The more it happens, the less people will trust your words.

Often, we make over-the-top statements when we're on the defensive. During their monthly review, my sales managers would often make grandiose promises when their performance was below the target. The more impressive the promises, the higher likelihood they would not accomplish them.

Once you become aware of consistently walking your talk, you will be attuned to any hypocrisy that creeps in. Rest assured, others will notice this quality in you, too.

## What Is a Promise?

Walking the talk means keeping promises. *Promise* is a loaded word. It may be assumed any time there is some sort of agreement. Alternatively, it's easy to just assume no promise was given if something was vaguely stated.

Your upbringing may have taught you to avoid certain promises. Do you remember as kids when, if someone didn't say the word "promise," that would excuse his or her double-crossing behavior?

I remember my daughters told me that a pinky promise, where you link your pinkies together, was a really strong promise. That kind of kid argument is full of mischief, because it means that other promises are up for interpretation and negotiation. This kid-like thinking shows up in our adult life. We package our promises into varying degrees of commitments.

I'm going to make this tough on you, but very simple: everything you say is a promise. Going even further:

- A promise is anything you say.

- A promise is anything you don't refute.

- A promise may be heard by your silence.

- A promise is done on time.

- A promise is when someone else promises something and you're part of that team.

- A promise is when you heard part of an issue but did not or could not hear the rest.

These are hardline definitions, so they remove any doubt about the value of your word. The rules are simple, but not easy, like all the things that make us better. When you follow this clear mandate about promises, you will quickly develop a reputation as a rock-solid, responsible person—the kind of person destined to lead.

A caveat to these rules is that promises can be managed and negotiated, but only through effective, timely communication.

Let's say somebody asks you to complete a task by next Friday, and you agree. Once you get back to your desk, you remember that you have many other tasks due by next Friday. You'll have to postpone. The time to go back to this person is immediately, not close to the deadline. If you wait too long to go back to this coworker, or if you say, "I couldn't get it done because I had these other two things to do," that's not managing your promises on time.

You may not be able to keep every promise you initially agree to, but you can manage them.

## When Are You Responsible?

Imagine you are in a meeting, and someone starts talking about a project. "We have to get this done by next week—" but just then you are called away and don't hear how the discussion turned out. You don't know if anyone was assigned or not.

It's almost too easy to tell yourself, "No one assigned me to a task. I didn't volunteer and no one mentioned me before I left." But from a leader's perspective, if you weren't clear that you're *not* handling it, you're on.

People who have worked directly for me know this all too well. If you heard something and you now know or suspect there's work to be done, you're responsible for participating in the work.

Projects and assignments will not always be spoon-fed to you. They may not even be explained clearly, and you may not fully understand your role. Getting to the heart of an issue can be like following a trail of breadcrumbs. If you know or suspect there's an issue, follow the trail.

I had an eccentric university professor who handed

out several assignments during the course that made up a significant part of our grade. He never scheduled or announced the assignments. They would just appear on his bulletin board.

All through the semester, my classmates and I had to keep checking his bulletin board to see if there was an assignment. We took turns checking and keeping others informed. It taught us that we were responsible for figuring out what we had to do. We couldn't rely on being told or assigned; if we missed an assignment, it was our fault.

One of the things I like to remind people, especially those in sales, is that God gave us two ears and one mouth. Ears are our reminder of the percentage of time we should be listening versus talking. When you do speak, ask open-ended questions to get clarity and understanding.

Be the person who ensures there is active listening. If you suspect an issue, slow down. Make sure it's not glossed over. Clarify who has the responsibility for action, because otherwise it's you!

Assuming responsibility in this way is really about taking initiative to solve a problem. By taking on this challenge in a proactive way, you naturally take on the role of a leader.

## A Promise Made Is a Promise Kept

If you notice someone lie to you just once, how long does it take before you can trust what that person says? It's quite a while, right? Failing to walk the talk is a variation of lying. It quickly destroys trust and respect.

People want to trust a leader, just like children want to trust consistency from a parent, the person they depend upon. Leaders who walk the talk create a safe, trusting environment because everyone knows how to behave and what to expect. Employee satisfaction goes up, too.

If you want to act as a leader, or if you hold a leadership position, you'll be called on to make some tough decisions. Staying true to your words makes these tough decisions easier for everyone involved. Personally, I think it's an extremely satisfying feeling.

The last principle—owning the end result—can be seen as an extension of walking the talk. In the next chapter, we will think more broadly about the promises your organization has made and how you can play a vital role in keeping those promises.

*Chapter 4*

# OWN THE END RESULT

"The most common way people give up their power is by thinking they don't have any."

—Alice Walker

## Sweat the Big Stuff

Imagine you're on the operating table having open-heart surgery.

A whole team of people stands around you: the anesthesiologist, the surgeon, interns, nurses, and visiting doctors. One nurse makes sure no sweat from the surgeon's face drops into your open heart; this is her only job.

What do you think this nurse's end result should be?

People in my workshops usually say it's that no sweat gets into the patient's wound.

As a patient, however, what's the end result you want? I'd imagine it's that you live!

But if that nurse pads the surgeon's forehead and keeps the sweat off the surgery area, she's doing her job, right?

Let's imagine this nurse at happy hour at the end of the day. She tells her friend, "You wouldn't believe what a wonderful job I did today. I went through two boxes of gauze pads, and I made sure not a single drop of sweat fell into the patient's body."

Her friend responds, "Wow, that's a lot of gauze. Why did you use so much?"

"Well, the surgeon was sweating profusely, because—can you believe this—he was totally drunk!"

"Oh my gosh, what happened to the patient?"

"Oh, he died. But listen, not a single drop of sweat fell on him!"

This is an over-the-top example of a mindset problem I see often: people focused only on their own task. As the patient, you want that nurse to say, "Doctor, you can't operate in your condition. We're not doing this surgery!"

You want her to own the end result.

## Your Job Is More Than Process

Finish this statement: Own the end result, not just

_____.

Not just your part? Not just what you want to do? Here's how most people complete this statement, and I agree: own the end result, not just the process.

A process-oriented person thinks, *I know the tasks that my job performs, and that's all I do. If I notice something's not working, it's out of my scope to do something about it.* Emerging leaders, even in low-level positions, never own just the process. They own the final outcome. This sets them apart from the pack and makes them much more valuable to their organization.

Maybe you flip hamburgers, and they later get assembled with all the condiments and the bun. You hear customers saying the meat is always cold. Would you stay quiet or take action, even if it's as simple as speaking up with recommendations?

I would argue that it's tough to be satisfied with your job if you know that the end result is not good. And it's tough on the business if your customers are not happy.

If you are part of a team, it means you own the responsibilities for the whole team. The nurse in the heart surgery story was part of a team. In sports, the most successful teams are ones where everyone contributes to winning the game, not just the superstar.

A lot of good jobs focus solely on process. Sometimes that's even in the job title, like mail processor or claims processor. Within these jobs, there's a greater challenge to break out of your specific task and shine as a leader. But it's still possible.

It's important that everyone do the process he or she is responsible for. The nurse in the operating room, wiping the surgeon's face, has to do her job. She can't do the surgeon's or the anesthesiologist's job. But she can own the whole end result.

If you are the mail processor and no mail is coming to the inbox for you to process, something is wrong. Your boss probably has a problem that she doesn't know about. You can influence the end result by sounding the alarm and escalating the issue to your boss or to whoever owns the total end result.

Giving yourself responsibility for the larger outcome in your organization is a recipe for creativity, proactivity, and leadership. Once you shift your mindset to own the larger outcome, you'll be amazed at all the inventive ways you maneuver through obstacles. Without this attitude, it's easy to fall into a narrow-minded, complacent approach.

## Commit without Conditions

Surprises and unexpected events happen in any organization, any group, anywhere. If you're ready to think beyond your own job, then you'll be able to make a difference when there is need.

If the hospital's power goes out and its generators fail, the patient on the operating table doesn't want to hear, "We can't complete this operation without any electricity. This one will have to die."

If you're waiting for someone else to direct you, then you are responsible for the patient dying on the table.

It's a matter of believing that you have the capability and ingenuity to make a difference. Yes, perhaps nothing can be done, but believing something could be done creates the opportunities for surprising results. Anyone have a phone flashlight?

You have probably encountered people who give only a conditional sort of commitment. "So long as she does her part, and he does his part, then I'll do my part." That's not leadership. Instead, make your mentality, *We'll get it done, regardless of the obstacles.*

Extraordinary things happen when leaders commit without conditions.

In 1962, when President Kennedy declared that we were going to the moon before the end of the 1960s, NASA agreed to make that dream happen. But when NASA made that commitment, two important metals had not yet been invented. Without these metals, the space capsule would burn up upon reentry. NASA didn't say, "We will get to the moon by the end of the decade so long as we can produce these two metals."

In fact, the inventions happened, and NASA did get to the moon before the end of the decade. No excuses, no transferring blame, and no conditions. NASA kept a clear focus on the end result.

This belief in our own ingenuity can serve us well. We are all quite capable of getting creative, especially under pressure. It has been said that during World War II, between 1940 and 1945, there were more inventions registered in the United States than between 1900 and 1940.

When you're committed to an end result, great progress happens.

## Sometimes a Nudge Is All You Need

When I was promoted to general manager of ComputerLand, one of my new responsibilities was oversight of the accounting department. A regional manager called me soon after my promotion to say that it was taking six to seven weeks for our sales reps to get their expenses reimbursed. Their credit card bills were often overdue. I agreed to look into it.

When I located the lady who handled the travel expenses, I asked her what her target goals were for turnaround.

"If I get the signed expense statement by Monday, I have the money in the employee's account by that Thursday." She proudly stated that she hadn't missed a target deadline yet.

"But I'm hearing that it's taking six to seven weeks before the people are reimbursed, so what's going on?"

She explained that the expense statements sat at the distribution center for a few days and then went to the desks of the vice presidents, where they sat for weeks at a time before being signed. Her process began after the statements were signed and delivered to her desk.

I sympathized with her frustration, but I asked her

to shift her mindset. "Your new timeline begins not when you receive the signed expense statement, but when the statement first comes into the distribution center."

She looked panic-stricken. "Wait a minute, I don't have control over the distribution center and the VPs!"

"I'll support you in whatever you need," I told her. "I agree these are real problems, and I'm looking for your help. I'll write any policy you want in order to make your targets happen. It's that important. Just think about it and get back to me."

Soon after that conversation, I traveled to a multi-day conference and got busy with my other priorities. A few weeks later, that same regional manager called me up and said, "We submitted the expense reports last week and we've already received the expense checks. Thanks for solving the problem."

Next, the VP of sales came by my office. "Who is this lady in accounts payable? She has my assistant trained not to give me any mail until I sign off on the sales reps' expense reports!"

A couple of weeks later, I had a meeting with all of my VPs, and they started talking about this accounts payable clerk, the new procedures, and something about red folders. Their assistants didn't even give them their plane tickets until they signed the expense statements. They were astounded by these changes that seemed to come from an accounts payable clerk.

I said to the group, "You know, we have an opening for the manager of the accounts payable department. I think I just found her!"

All this clerk needed was a small event—a supervisor sharing a problem with her—to give her new, big-picture goals.

I did not write any policy for her. She did not ask for my approval on a new procedure. She just acted, working toward her target. She invented her own system, including red folders that would stand out in the distribution center. She created a new procedure for each VP's assistant to follow.

It still gives me such pleasure when I think about this woman's out-of-the-box thinking and determination to achieve her goal. Her visibility in the organization skyrocketed as a result of her proactive approach. And she got a promotion, too!

The lesson here is that we can get so much done if we own the end result, not just our portion of the work.

## Leaders Own the End Result

A follower thinks things happen to him or her. A leader makes things happen. When people own the end result, others say, "I want you to follow that person." Leaders are defined by who wants to follow them—nothing else.

Many of us have learned that as long as we give a good effort or have a really good excuse, we're okay if a project fails. For a leader, the challenge is to think that's not okay. Even if you could never achieve the end result, for whatever reason, it's far better to have tried and learned from your experience.

As the CEO of a company, my job was to care about the whole, but I couldn't notice everything. I always wanted my employees to care about the whole, too, so they could be my eyes, ears, and brains on the ground, making things work. I wanted to hire employees who owned the end result, not just their specific task.

This third principle is all-encompassing and can color your approach to every project you touch. Now that you've got that one under your belt, let's explore how the benefits of practicing these principles expand to enrich your personal and professional life.

*Chapter 5*

# LEADERSHIP IN ACTION

"The only person you are destined to become is the person you decide to be."

—Ralph Waldo Emerson

## Principles for Life

Now that you've implemented at least one, and hopefully more, of these principles, you should be seeing and feeling a difference in your work life.

Do coworkers treat you with greater respect? Has your boss paid you a compliment or given you a larger responsibility? Do you feel more invested in your job?

Sometimes, the greatest reward comes from the new way you perceive yourself. If you've been the quiet hero of your organization, catching arrows, walking your talk, and owning the end result, I'll bet you feel pretty great about yourself. And you should! Living by these principles requires dedication, courage, and will. If you are making this effort, that in itself is truly admirable. The good results will follow.

Most people I've worked with come to me looking for help advancing their careers. They implement the principles and get the satisfaction that comes from being a leader in their workplace. But then something else happens that they weren't expecting: their personal lives improve.

It may have occurred to you already that these principles are rules to live by, not just guidelines for the workplace. When you practice them at the office, the new behaviors manifest in other places, too. Once you start acting like a leader, that behavior becomes part of your identity.

You will begin to see how this new mentality infuses your personal life with a positive energy. You take on personal challenges—from getting the kids to school on time to making your health a priority—with greater focus, ingenuity, and accountability.

Families, sports teams, volunteer groups, and social groups all need leaders. And by this I don't mean they need someone to boss them around! I mean that they need people who live by the three principles. The world could use more people who catch arrows, walk their talk, and own end results.

As you implement these principles in your life, I have one final piece of advice: go the extra mile to ensure your outcomes. All the best planning in the world can't replace a successful result.

## Protect Your Outcomes

Many of us work diligently to achieve an end result, but we take the work right to the edge, assuming too much risk. We believe things will go according to plan and fail to enact measures that safeguard the outcome.

Here's an illustration of what I mean. Let's say your sister tells you a couple of weeks before her wedding that she'd like you to help with the cake.

You say, "No problem! Tell me about the cake you want."

"I can make it really easy for you. Here's a picture of the cake. My friend had it at her wedding a couple of weeks ago, and it was delicious. I found the baker who made it. Here's the name and address. I'd like a slightly different icing color to match the bridesmaids' dresses, and I need it at the reception hall on my wedding day by 10:00 a.m. Can you do it?"

You tell her you'd be happy to help. You go the bakery, meet the owner, and describe the wedding cake. You show him the cake photo, and he recognizes it from the wedding a few weeks ago. He confirms he can make the cake with that icing color. You give him the specific date, time, and address.

He tells you, "Consider it done. I'm the best baker in town. I've been in business for twenty-one years, and I have not missed a single delivery. You see all these awards on the wall? I won all of them. I make the best cake and provide the best service in town."

You may be thinking, *What an easy job*. You were planning to go away on a two-week vacation, coming home on an overnight flight on the day before the wedding. It shouldn't be a problem, because the baker will have the cake there right at 10:00 a.m. Easy!

Would you go ahead with your vacation plans and arrive the morning of the wedding?

I wouldn't. Trusting that things will go according to plan works only in best-case scenarios. We're not living in an ideal world. You always have to prepare for the worst to protect your outcome.

If I were in charge of the wedding cake, I'd postpone

my vacation—and more. After all, this is your sister, and she plans on being married just once.

Here's what I suggest. You change the way you drive to work to make sure that the baker is still operating and the lights are on. You pop your head in to say hello every few days.

You visit the bakery to the point where the owner considers filing a restraining order against you. You have a second baker make a cake too, just in case. Perhaps you buy a few cake mixes and on Friday night before the wedding make a back-up cake. It may not look pretty, but it's a guaranteed cake.

From my perspective, there has to be zero chance that something goes wrong.

But let's say you don't heed my advice, and you take that vacation. On Saturday morning, you drive by the bakery on the way to the wedding. A van from the Health and Safety Department is parked outside, and yellow tape criss-crosses the door. A sign says, "Closed due to salmonella contamination."

Of course, at the wedding, everybody notices the cake is missing. Through her tears, your sister says she totally understands.

In her photo album, pictures show an empty table with a sign: "We apologize, no wedding cake." For the rest of your life, whenever you go to a family event that has a cake, people joke, "Hey, this is what a cake looks like."

The consequences ripple out to the next generations. At family gatherings, your offspring are seated at the kids' table. They're the loser part of the family who couldn't provide a cake for a wedding. By now, they've forgotten the details; they just know that your family couldn't deliver.

## Let Them Eat Cake

In an alternate version of the story, just days before the wedding you find out that there has been an outbreak of "mad flour disease." Flour all across the country is contaminated. Now people are buying ice cream cakes, but it's summer and the cakes are melting at weddings. It's just awful.

During this widespread cake crisis, you walk into the reception hall with a traditional flour cake. When people ask how you did it, you don't say. Remember the travel agency and the snowstorm? It's not about how you did it; it's that you got it done.

This is what you secretly know: Once it was discovered that cakes in this country were contaminated, you spent all the money you had saved for your vacation on a ticket to Paris. You bought a gorgeous, uncontaminated Parisian cake and flew home with the confection safely on the seat next to you.

Everyone is so happy about that cake; it's the only cake in the country! It makes the wedding an extraordinary day, filled with magic and blessings. The press finds out, and the story is written up in *People*, *Time*, and elsewhere.

Now, for ten generations afterward, your offspring sit at the head table. They are known as the hero branch of the family. Their ancestor delivered the only cake in the country. A cake was delivered, and a promise was kept.

When you take your outcome for granted, you diminish your chances for success. You know your end result is in jeopardy if you hear youself saying some variation of:

- "I've handled it already; it will be fine."
- "Someone else is taking care of it."

When the worst does happen, it can be tempting to blame the forces beyond your control. Your response might be:

- "I couldn't help it."

- "That's just the way it is."

It's so much more effective and empowering to go the extra mile to protect your outcomes. The mindset of accomplishing a goal no matter what fosters extraordinary responsibility and ingenuity. This is one of many ways that following the three principles creates leadership attributes.

## See Yourself Become a Leader

As an executive looking for my next hire, I want a person whose attitudes and actions demonstrate all of the three principles. I want someone who acts with courage and is willing to "take the hit" for the organization. I look for a person with integrity who thinks about the ultimate outcome and makes it happen.

None of us wants to be the maintenance guy on the deck of the Titanic who says, "Look, my job was rearranging the deck chairs. Yeah, I saw the iceberg, but that wasn't my job."

That's not a way to feel good about yourself (or, in his case, stay alive).

I think we'd all rather be the person who, to some

degree, is noticed by others in a positive way. The one who makes things happen. A person who gets talked about like this:

- "What you see is what you get. Her word is good."
- "Give that project to him; he'll get it done."
- "Give her the team; she will keep everyone accountable."
- "He's resourceful and never lets anything drop."
- "Whatever she tells you, you know she will deliver."
- "I can always trust him to keep his promises, no matter what."

To me, all these statements say "leader." Anyone can be that person. Remember, I achieved my success based on what I did, not who I am.

Once you work through the three principles, you'll notice that you naturally begin to accumulate more and more leadership qualities. When you catch the arrows, walk your talk, and own the end result, people will begin to see you as confident, innovative, and risk-taking—three of the leadership attributes from chapter 1.

The more you work at putting the principles into practice, the more leadership qualities you'll develop.

## Join a Community of Leaders

I have used these principles in my work life, in my personal life, and as a consultant and mentor. Feel free to email me at <u>CR@CatchTheArrows.com</u> if you have questions or if you or your organization would like help instilling these principles in your staff.

So, my friends, go and shine. Practice these three principles every opportunity you get. Remember that a journey happens in steps, so don't be discouraged if the change doesn't happen overnight. Being on the right path ensures the right outcome. You have the direction you need.

It's time to take that path and become the leader you've always wanted to be.

# ABOUT THE AUTHOR

Chandran began his career at IBM, where he spent fourteen years in sales, marketing, and management roles. For the next five years, he oversaw the expansion of ComputerLand Canada, a computer retailer from 17 stores to 76 stores. Appointed president and CEO at Gestetner Corp in 1991, he engineered that company's turnaround from a loss position to one of an annually increasing profit.

In 1997, he joined PC software and hardware reseller Softchoice Corporation as president and CEO.

With his unique and effective brand of leadership, Chandran orchestrated remarkable sales growth from $70m in 1997 to over $500m in 2001. He capped his corporate career in 2008 as an executive at Dell Inc.

Chandran now concentrates full time on consulting with companies and coaching individuals. Through his three principles of leadership, he teaches people how to excel, become leaders, and get recognized at work. He shares his passion for empowering employees and "delighting" customers with seminars and workshops throughout North America. He's seen these principles work for both high-level executives and entry-level sales reps.

A Sri Lankan immigrant with modest beginnings, Chandran achieved success in life through what he did, not who he was. He believes that leadership traits can be learned by anyone. His system has helped thousands of people achieve the results they want at work and in life for more than thirty years.

Chandran and his wife Holli live in Salem OR They have 6 daughters and stepdaughters  and 9 grandchildren.

# Schedule Chandran to Speak at Your Next Event

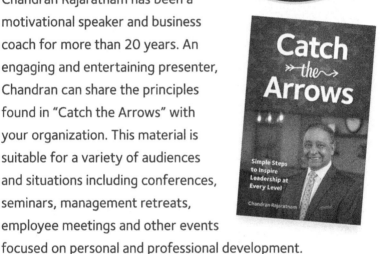

Chandran Rajaratnam has been a motivational speaker and business coach for more than 20 years. An engaging and entertaining presenter, Chandran can share the principles found in "Catch the Arrows" with your organization. This material is suitable for a variety of audiences and situations including conferences, seminars, management retreats, employee meetings and other events focused on personal and professional development.

## Outcomes

When people who attend these seminars embrace Chandran's principles, organizations reap the rewards through:

- Improved individual leadership
- Enhanced management effectiveness
- Stronger teams
- Sustained growth in sales performance

**Audience members will leave inspired, revitalized and encouraged to reach their full potential.**

## Reviews

"Chandran has been a great business advisor for my company. His 'Principles for Effective Teams' has become a guiding strategy for our management team. Before we make any major decisions, we work through those principles."

   -Kelly Yunker, President, PES

"The content of the session was perfectly aligned with our needs, covering the fundamentals of leadership through to practical implementation and guidelines, and the initiation of an entire company framework for managing and encouraging the best performance from all our employees. It is quite unlike the typical leadership 'BS' sessions that are all too common in the training industry. Completely refreshing and uplifting."

   -Dominick Garton, President & CEO, Clyde Bergemann Inc.

"Chandran taught us that as leaders our first goal has to be to do those things that only we can do for the organization. He also taught us to "manage to end results." I can say without fear of contradiction that our lives, our business and our futures are all considerably enriched from his teachings and concepts."

   -Dwayne Thomas, Past President, Hollywood Lighting

### Contact Chandran Today!
Chandran can be reached at:
CR@CatchtheArrows.com
971.599.5142

Made in United States
Orlando, FL
08 March 2024